IT'S A BIRTHDAY SUIT

Bil Keane

FAWCETT GOLD MEDAL ● NEW YORK

A Fawcett Gold Medal Book
Published by Ballantine Books
Copyright © 1984 by Register and Tribune Syndicate, Inc.
Copyright © 1980 by Register and Tribune Syndicate, Inc.

Library of Congress Catalog Card Number: 84-90929

ISBN 0-449-12420-7

Manufactured in the United States of America

First Edition: December 1984

10 9 8 7 6 5 4 3 2 1

"Whose birthday is next, Mommy?"

"There! Now run along outside and get some
fresh air in your lungs."

"If you and Jeffy sing with me, we'll have a three-o."

"What are 'Britches', Mommy? Grandma says
I'm getting too big for mine."

"I'm tryin' to play a game with PJ, but he keeps acting like a baby!"

"Daddy, why don't you take the other half of
your doughnut for recess?"

"I'm Jeffy. Stop callin' me Linus!"

"I have a paring knife, a plastic fork, and a
tablespoon. Who set the . . . ."

"Don't turn on the darkness yet."

"I wish they'd have put the extra day in the summer."

"Hearts, hearts! I'm sick of drawin' hearts."

"This car has 10,000 miles on it. It was made in Hong Kong."

"If you use our bathroom the little round soaps in a jar are just to look at."

"Daddy's almost awake. Shall I wake him all the way?"

"I'm writing a story, but I can't think of what to put after 'Once Upon A Time.'"

"Finders keepers, losers weepers! Saint
Anthony said that."

"Daddy isn't here. His boss kept him
after work."

"Guess what happened at school today!
Britain invaded Ethiopia, Pearl Harbor was
bombed, and Roosevelt declared war
on Japan!"

"Say something
to grandma."

"My birthday is
next week."

"Daddy, can I watch the newspaper
with you?"

"Which kind of spice am I made out of?"

"You have to do that when you're married."

"Cookie Monster my foot! I know who the
Cookie Monster is around this house!"

"This flake doesn't have any sugar on it."

"Billy has to stay in his room. He's been taking
after your side of the family again."

"Not too rough with them right after dinner."

"I had a neat dream last night. I hope it's a mini-series."

"This one's mine. It grew faster 'cause I talk to it a lot."

"Hereafter, always take the lollipop out of your mouth before you kiss daddy."

"They left too much space between the raisins."

"Grandma's allowed to watch a lot 'cause they didn't have TV when she was a kid."

"The wind keeps tryin' to get in!"

"Our art teacher was in charge today. Her
name's O'Reilly."

"They're tickets for the supermarket."

"We've got a customer, Mommy!"

"I heard somebody say 'Heeeeeeere's Johnny!'"

"I hope you wear it out before I hafta grow into it."

"Billy said he was too sick to go to school, so Mommy's giving him the lie detector test."

"But wolves can't talk."

"I like radio better than TV 'cause the picture doesn't flip."

"Cruise straight on down Central, Grandma . . ."
"Hang a left at the second light . . ."
"Jump on the freeway at the interchange . . . ."

"We're going to take a vote to see if we all go out for pizza."

"AVRIL FOOLS!"

"Daddy's going to fill out the census question-
naire so we all hafta stand still while
he counts us."

"Yes, Mommy, I hung them up."

"Mommy, will you help me write a letter to the Easter Bunny?"

"I like this better than Halloween. You don't
have to go all over the neighborhood."

"I have a headache, I'd better take a couple of jelly beans."

"Would you mind withdrawing your troops from my chair?"

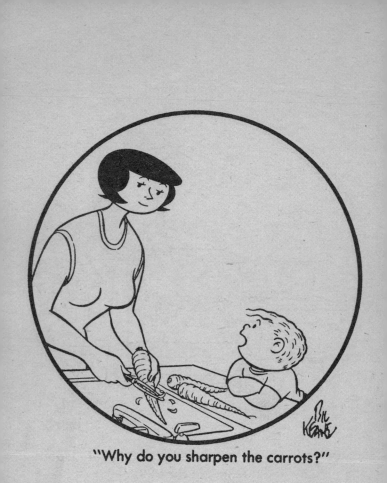

"Why do you sharpen the carrots?"

"Well, actually, y'see I spotted this puddle in
Ferrell's driveway and I . . . well,
I just lost my head."

"If you fall and break your neck there'll be no TV for you tonight!"

"Am I adding and subtracting too loud for you?"

"Come take your nap like a big boy."
"Big boys don't take naps."

"Mommy, I need my ruler and it's holding up
your bedroom window."

"You know what broccoli is, Jeffy. It's those little trees."

"They made me class treasurer. I was the only
one with change for a dollar."

"Mommy always ties them double. Have you learned to do that yet?"

"When will PJ speak English instead of Babyish?"

"Mommy, these flowers want to get up out of the dirt."

"What ELSE needs painting?"

"Gee, Mommy, I'm not gonna perform an operation — I'm just gonna have lunch."

"When the sun sets how far down does it go?"

"At school we learned what the two holes in your nose are called. They're nozzles."

"Look at that car, Mommy. They took the lid off."

"Don't cut my sideburns."

"How'd you like a nickel sammich?"

"I smell paint."

"Kathy's mother is pregnant, Mommy. Were you ever pregnant?"

"Daddy's taking his tennis trophy to work for
Show-and-Tell."

"Aren't you going to put any water in?"

"Was there an older generation when you were little, Mommy?"

"Listen, Daddy. I'll hit you a song."

"Breakfast is ready for the rest of the week. I need the box for a project."

"I didn't know pasghetti came in sticks."

"I have to find the common denominator."
"Want me to help you look for it?"

"Sam sneezed, Mommy. Do we God bless doggies?"

"Did you say thank you to Mrs. Nagurny?"
"Couldn't. In the middle of the party she ran
away from home."

"I didn't know our car had a sword."

"That's OK. Daddy'll fix it tonight."

"Now pitch me a knuckle ball."

"Can Charlie stay for lunch?"
"That depends. Which one is Charlie?"

"I hope we're gettin' that sitter who lets us stay up to watch Johnny Carson."

"Grandma said I'm very nautical today and I was
tryin' to be good!"

"Look! Our table has a sun roof!"

"That isn't dust. It's cinnamon!"

"Susan's in a family way."   "That means she's pregnant."

"Hi, Daddy! I was just showing Jeffy how I can reach the doorbell now."

"Another sad ending. He has to kiss the girl."

"I saw this on TV, and now they've got it in a book."

"Can I go outside for a couple of whiles?"

"I don't care for any of that ketchup juice."

"What is it we're about to receive?"

"Why do WE hafta go to bed when Mommy
gets tired?"

"We learned about that in sex ed."

"Mommy, can you get my pants loose from the bike chain?"

"The milk goes on the first floor of the
refrigerator and the ice cream goes upstairs."

"Mommy! Y'know the bubble gum Billy lost?
Well, I found it!"

"Happy Father's Day, Daddy! Daddy? Happy
Father's Day! DADDY! . . . Shall we
open it for you?"

"The glass wasn't big enough for what I poured."

"Daddy says after he grew up his old back-
yard got littler. I can't see
ours shrinkin' any."

"Tell Billy to stop callin' me Miss Piggy!"

"Let's wait for another bus, Mommy. All the
windows are taken on this."

"Don't move, Daddy. We're playin' hide-and-seek
and you're my hidin' place."

"Do you know 'Look for the Union Label'?"

"Look, Daddy! They even give us doggy bags!"

"For the last time shut that darn thing off and
let's go sightseeing!"

"Can we go in there and see if our senators are doin' any work?"

"Was Abraham Lincoln really that big?"

"This isn't a vacation. It's just like our American
history class in school."

"This is my favorite historical site, Daddy,
'cause we get to ride the elevator."

"Can we go back up there again, Daddy? I told grandma I'd wave to her but I forgot."

"Oh, no! The White House is closed Mondays!"

"Know why, Daddy? It's the day the first lady
hasta do her housecleaning."

"The policemen ride horses 'cause it saves gasoline."

"Why do they call 'em Memorials? They're nothin' but buildings."

"Another thing I like about Washington is their yummy food and neat places to eat."

"Did the Smif'sonian people get the idea for that castle from Disneyland?"

"Jeffy touched the command module!"

"Why didn't you go before we got on?"

"I guess the president's kids keep their swings
and things out in the BACK yard."

"Quiet, PJ! If the president is takin' a nap and you wake him up you're gonna get it!"

"Why are those men fighting over that flag?"

"Do ya think maybe we can fly home on Air
Force One?"

"The things I like to smell best are flowers, Mommy's perfume and pastrami."

"Won't the soap be bad for my goldfish?"